GLORY IN SACRIFICE

By the same author:

Crucify all ambition
Bury all Individualism

ASHBURNHAM INSIGHTS:
   Baptism in Holy Spirit
   Blessing and Cursing
   Counselling
   Deliverance
   Healing
   Intercession
   Prophecy
   Tongues and Explanations

Glory in Sacrifice

TIMOTHY PAIN

KINGSWAY PUBLICATIONS

EASTBOURNE

British Library Cataloguing in Publication Data

Pain, Timothy
    Glory in Sacrifice.
    1. Bible—Expositions
    I. Title II. Series
    220.6

    ISBN 0-86065-709-4

Production and printing in Great Britain for
KINGSWAY PUBLICATIONS LTD
Lottbridge Drove, Eastbourne, E Sussex BN23 6NT by
Nuprint Ltd, Harpenden, Herts AL5 4SE

This trilogy was inspired by three of the many Christian leaders who have moulded my life. Two of their lives made me start asking the serious questions which lie behind these books. The life of the third man pointed me towards the answer.

This trilogy is dedicated to that man, the Rt Revd Peter Ball, who personifies the principles set out in these three books more than any other man I know.

Contents

The death of Self

Lord, when the sense of Thy sweet grace
Sends up my soul to seek Thy face,
Thy blessed eyes breed such desire,
I die in Love's delicious fire.
    O Love, I am thy sacrifice;
Be still triumphant, blessed eyes;
Still shine on me, fair suns, that I
Still may behold, though still I die.

Though still I die, I live again;
Still longing so to be still slain;
So gainful is such loss of breath;
I die even in desire of death.
    Still live in me this loving strife
Of living death and dying life;
For while Thou sweetly slayest me
Dead to myself, I live in Thee.

A Song of Divine Love
Richard Crashaw

Introduction

When I began writing this trilogy I thought that the material would form volumes nine to twelve in the developing *Ashburnham Insights* series. I set out to write four short books on vision, community, worship, and service, intending to suggest in them that God wants to move us on from personal to corporate renewal, and that we should join Paul in asking to share in the sufferings of Christ as well as in the power of his resurrection. But somewhere between conception and parturition God, and an editor, intervened.

The first eight volumes in the *Ashburnham Insights* series were my attempt at a serious re-reading of Scripture on topics which, currently, are immensely popular. But as I began preparing this new material I realised that I was now focusing on subjects which people prefer to ignore.

When the material for volumes one to eight in the *Ashburnham Insights* was tested in public it received an enthusiastic welcome: some folk may have struggled with small details, but most people endorsed the general principles. However, I am afraid that this new material has gone down everywhere like the proverbial lead balloon.

One summer's evening in 1987, after a particularly violent and antagonistic reception at a Shropshire Bible

Week, I decided that enough was enough. I could not face any more vituperation and decided to ditch the material. But a few quiet words of encouragement and endorsement on the following day from the Rev Frank Cooke gave me the determination to press on and begin pounding my word-processor. So blame Frank if you find this trilogy unpalatable!

I prepared some rough manuscripts, sent them to my editor, and then flew to South Africa where I spent a month living with black clergymen, teaching them, visiting their congregations, and tasting apartheid at first-hand. It was a deeply challenging experience. After South Africa I spent some time in Northern Ireland. And it was there, gazing at the poppy-clad memorial to *Our Glorious Dead* in bomb-scarred Enniskillen, that I began to perceive the common theme which ran through my rough manuscripts.

I arrived home from Ireland to find an encouraging letter from my editor. He stated that some people would be so unhappy with what I had written, and find it so unwelcome, that he didn't know what to do with the manuscripts. After prayer, thought, reflection and discussion we finally agreed not to include this material in the *Ashburnham Insights*, but to develop it into the format of this trilogy.

I belong to that part of the church which is unashamedly both evangelical and charismatic. But in South Africa I was appalled to discover that apartheid appears to have as strong a grip on the lives of evangelical charismatics as it does on members of the armed forces. Certainly that is the view of most of the black Baptist clergymen with whom I stayed in the Transvaal townships.

It would have been easy for me to return home and denounce the white-led charismatic mega-churches of Johannesburg. But I suspected that if I had grown up there I would probably have been part of them, for they emphasised many of the things I hold most dear. They were not bad, but blind. They had a splinter called apartheid in both eyes. And I realised that if I was to take Matthew 7:5 seriously I needed to identify and remove the plank in my own eye before I could do anything about their splinter. That is what I have tried to do in this trilogy.

Books One and Two are my prayerful attempts at identifying the two critical planks which I believe seriously distort my vision and the vision of many other evangelical and charismatic leaders and congregations today. Book Three is my prescription for a course of treatment which might improve our vision, and so set us free to remove our brothers' splinters.

Whereas the *Ashburnham Insights* were written primarily for house-group leaders as hand-books for house-group study, *The death of Self* has been written especially for ministers, and I have primarily had a congregational application in mind. Of course I hope that these three books will also be widely used as a stimulating basis for a series of house-group meetings, but I particularly urge all in 'full-time Christian service' to work slowly through the trilogy, allowing the scorching light of Scripture to penetrate their presuppositions and experiences.

I am not a theologian. I am not even the full-time minister of a particular congregation. I'm just a man who has looked in his mirror and asked God to show him his planks. I have not attempted to construct watertight arguments to convince the staunchest doubter. Instead I've tried to pose questions which need careful thought; to propose omissions in our teaching; to point out imbalances in our emphases; and to plead that holy self-effacement and humble sacrifice may predominate in our personal, congregational and denominational lives.

I am sure that I must have got many things wrong. Even Paul admitted that his knowledge was imperfect. My problem is that I don't know what I'm wrong about; I doubt if I am the only person with this particular problem. Whilst I acknowledge it is unlikely that anybody will agree with everything in this trilogy, I do hope that everybody may be provoked and challenged by some part of each book.

Please read the books in the suggested order, and take care to look up all the Scripture references as you proceed through the text. Unless otherwise indicated, my biblical quotations are taken from the Jerusalem Bible.

My thanks go to all the members of both the Ashburnham Stable Family and the Ashburnham Parish Church for their unfailing patience, love and support. The following deserve special mention either for a contribution or for their company in a particularly formative experience: Ken Barham, Brian and Susan Betts, John and Marlis Bickersteth, Jean Breach, Teresa Clifton, Winifred Cox, David and Christine Freeland, Edmund Heddle, John Herbert, Sue Lindsay, Jo and Susie Marriott, Richard Martin, Margery May, Ralph May, Chris Nicholls, Jennifer Oldroyd, Alison Pain, David and Edna Parr, Catherine Rendall, and Roger and Penny Wilcock.

Timothy Pain

Glory in Sacrifice

Sometimes I wish that I might do
  Just one grand deed and die,
And by that one grand deed reach up
  To meet God in the sky.
But such is not Thy way, O God,
  Not such is Thy decree,
But deed by deed, and tear by tear,
  Our souls must climb to Thee,
As climbed the only Son of God
  From manger unto Cross,
Who learned, though tears and bloody sweat,
  To count this world but loss;
Who left the Virgin Mother's Arms
  To seek those arms of shame,
Outstretched upon the lonely hill
  To which the darkness came.
As deed by deed, and tear by tear,
  He climbed up to the height,
Each deed a splendid deed, each tear
  A jewel shining bright,
So grant us, Lord, the patient heart,
  To climb the upward way,
Until we stand upon the height,
  And see the perfect day.

Patience
G. A. Studdert Kennedy

Sacrifice
and
Glory

Better to die for Jesus than to live for self; better to bleed for Jesus than to preserve one's life wholly unsuffering. Oh crucify this church, nail us to His cross. Let us die with Him; let us slumber in His grave; and then let us wake up and live only in His resurrection.

Charles Spurgeon

Sacrifices are central to the Scriptures: from the unknown animals who provided the skins in the Garden of Eden, to the two Witnesses who gave their lives in the book of Revelation, sacrifices run through the Bible like letters in a stick of rock. Yet today sacrifice is a subject we prefer to ignore: for there will never be an appetite for sacrifice in the society or congregation which values ambition and individualism.

The cross is the place of supreme sacrifice, and, in all ages, on every continent, throughout all traditions, it has been continually recognised as the universal symbol of our Christian faith. In years past the content of hymns, the shape of buildings, the ornaments on altars and walls, the decorations of stained-glass windows, the brooches on lapels, all illustrated the centrality of the cross. Yet today less than one per cent of the 500 plus recently written *Songs of Fellowship* even mention the word 'cross', Good Friday has been relegated to the second division of religious festivals, and the dove and the fish have virtually usurped the place of the cross on charismatic collars. This final part of *The death of Self* trilogy is my plea for sacrifice to be better understood and given again its rightful place in the Christian life.

Another great scriptural theme is the glory of God.

And this, in stark contrast to sacrifice, is currently in vogue. Shouts of 'glory' are always heard at times of celebration; pleas for glory are commonly made in fervent times of prayer; and the word itself is a key ingredient in countless charismatic choruses. We want God to be glorified, and we want to experience his glory. But we forget that glory without sacrifice is impossible.

God's glory appeared to the seventy elders on Mount Sinai after sacrifice (Exodus 24); his glory was regularly seen in the wilderness tabernacle at the hour of sacrifice (Leviticus 9:6–24); and the only way into the tabernacle was at the altar of sacrifice (Exodus 40:29–35). God's glory filled the Jerusalem Temple, but only after innumerable sacrifices had been made (1 Kings 8:1–11). Jesus was always the outshining of God's glory (Hebrews 1:3), but his death on the cross was the supreme moment, this side of the Second Advent, of the revelation of God's glory (John 7:39; 12:23–28; 13:31; 17:5; Hebrews 2:9). And if we want to share in that same glory then we must also share in the sufferings of his sacrifice (Romans 8:18). The path of glory is the pavement of sacrifice. Only fools and heretics attempt to disentangle glory from sacrifice.

Glory is an onomatopoeic word; sacrifice is not. Glory sounds great in our mouths; sacrifice grates in our throats. Many think that glory means something nice or bright; most dismiss sacrifice as medieval or islamic. Both words are greatly misunderstood. Yet I believe that a right understanding and application of glory and sacrifice—and the relationship between them—is vital for the church today.

The Hebrew word for glory is *kabod*. It is occasionally used to describe the material prosperity, physical splendour or good reputation of men. Less commonly it poetically describes the warriors of a nation or the soul of a man. But *kabod* is normally reserved for God. In the Old Testament the expression *the glory of God* is used in two different ways. Firstly, it is a parallel term to *the name of God* and refers to the self-revealed character of God. And, secondly, it denotes a visible revelation to men of God's presence. God's glory shows men where he is and what he is like: it is the outward manifestation of his absolute holiness. In the New Testament these aspects of God's glory are perfectly fulfilled in Christ: he is both the complete self-revelation of God's character and also the clearest revelation of God's presence. Today it is the church's function both to show God's holy character to the world and to be seen by the world as the place where God resides.

The Greek word used in the New Testament for glory is *doxa*. This also sometimes refers to human honour, but it normally describes Jesus' revelation, by grace and by powerful deeds, of God's nature. *Doxa* adds to *kabod* the sense of a demonstration of beautiful perfection and a display of magnificent power. God's glory seen in Jesus shows the Father's splendid excellence and the full extent of his regal authority and power.

This glory was seen at the Cana wedding, John 2:1–12, when Jesus exhibited God's grace and power by turning water into vintage wine. This glory was visible at the Bethany cemetery when Lazarus was dramatically resuscitated, John 11:1–44. This glory shone at the Transfiguration, the Resurrection, and the Ascension. But it was never so bright as at Calvary, for there was seen the complete self-revelation of God's nature, the greatest possible demonstration of his grace and love, the supreme manifestation of his absolute holiness, and the perfect display of his excellent beauty, his majestic power, and his royal authority. Calvary was the most visible revelation, so far, of God's presence in the world: it was the quintessence of glory.

When, today, we pray for God's glory to be seen we are really asking that the world will see his holiness, his grace, and his power. But these can only be seen in the church. When we sing 'glorify your name' we are pleading, perhaps unwittingly, for God's character, God's beauty, and God's majesty to be unveiled to the world. Yet these can only be seen in the church and in creation. And when we cry 'glory' we are encapsulating all that God is into one word, and so should be shaking with awe because this word, this glory, is our destiny.

1 Corinthians 11:7 shows that man was made as the image and glory of God: that is, to be a complete revelation of God's nature and presence. We don't need Romans 3:23 to remind us how much we have fallen short of this glorious destiny; however, Jesus has fulfilled this destiny and, by his sacrifice, has made it possible for all men to experience and demonstrate this glory. Hebrews 2:6–10 says, 'We see in Jesus one who was for a short while made lower than the angels and is now crowned with glory and splendour *because he submitted to death*; by God's grace he had to experience death for all mankind. As it was his purpose to bring a great many of his sons into glory, it was appropriate that God, for whom everything exists and through whom everything exists, should make perfect, *through suffering*, the leader who would take them to their salvation.'

Jesus was glorified at the place of supreme sacrifice. It was there on the cross that he received a crown of great glory as the reward for his voluntary death. It was there that, by his loving sacrifice, he made it possible for us to see and to reflect God's glory, and to begin to be transformed into God's likeness with ever increasing glory. And, because of the cross, God's glory seen in the face of Jesus Christ can now be seen and be reflected by the church.

The Scriptures teach that this glory is especially shared now and in eternity by those who make sacrifices, voluntary and involuntary, with Christ: Romans 8:17–18; 2 Corinthians 4:1–18; and 1 Peter 4:13 all underline the link between glory and sacrifice; and the Sermon on the Mount stresses the glorious heavenly reward awaiting both those who deliberately sacrifice human acclaim, and those who go on enduring persecution because of Christ. In Matthew 6:1–16 Jesus categorically states that those who parade their good deeds before men to attract their notice lose all reward from their Father in heaven; and that those who publicise their generosity, or pray and worship ostentatiously, have had all the reward that they are going to get. Our love-inspired sacrifices are rewarded with heavenly holy glory. The congregational and personal ambitions we achieve are rewarded with earthly human acclaim and, sometimes, material prosperity. We choose, whether we realise it or not, between a human reward here-and-now and a divine reward hereafter. Those who cry out for glory must understand that before this can be attained they must have shared in the sufferings and sacrifice of Christ.

I believe that the scriptural teaching about sacrifice is greatly misunderstood. Many people have a general, but not a detailed, awareness of the Old Testament sacrifices. Nearly all believers know that Christ's once-and-for-all sacrifice ended the need for the ritual blood-sacrifices. And some people therefore erroneously conclude that the need for all sacrifices ended at the cross. But the Old Testament understanding of sacrifice is not restricted to ritual. And even the legal ceremonies are not just ancient rites, of interest only to aged professors; the principles they teach are so important, and their significance is so great, that all believers need to know about them.

Most people are aware of the New Testament references to spiritual sacrifices, yet some fail to understand these in the light of the Old Testament teaching about sacrifice. A few people reckon that every act of a Spirit-filled man can be deemed a spiritual sacrifice. Some believers who struggle with suffering grasp its vital relationship with sacrifices. Nearly all Christians know that our sacrifices cannot atone for our sin—only Christ's sacrifice does that; but only a minority perceive the relationship between his once-for-all sacrifice and his demand for his followers to live a life of continuous self-sacrifice.

This is a book about self-denial, self-death and self-sacrifice, for it seems to me that the Scriptures show that nothing reflects or attracts God's glory like sacrifice. I am sure that most believers desire glory. I realise that nearly all Christians long for their friends and relatives to glimpse God's glory. I hope that all readers want the whole world to see his glory. And I expect that you, like me in my more rational moments, realise that a heavenly reward must be preferable to human acclaim or material prosperity. If that is so, I ask you to join me in a brief biblical investigation into sacrifice, and then in a life-long embrace of the glory of God which is found only in sacrifice.

Sacrifice
in the
Old Testament

Sacrifice gives you no pleasure,
were I to offer holocaust, you would not have it.
My sacrifice is this broken spirit,
you will not scorn this crushed and broken heart.

King David

Sacrifice began with God. He made the first sacrifice. He spilt the first blood. He suffered the first loss. And his example established the pattern and principles for all future sacrifices. In Genesis 3:16–21 God offered the recently cursed Adam and Eve some replacement clothes. It is implicit in verse 21 that one or two animals died to provide the clothes; and surely it must have been God himself who slew, then skinned, some of those precious, perfect animals which only a short while before he had carefully made, lovingly blessed, and proudly described as good.

This little incident teaches much about Old Testament sacrifice. Those who benefited were completely undeserving. Those who suffered were totally blameless. The sacrifice was permanent: blood was shed, the animals would not be reincarnated. The sacrificial material was in perfect condition: only the very best would do for God. The cost was considerable, both for God and the animals; and the loss was absolute. Grace, love and mercy were the motivating emotions. The ones for whom the sacrifice was made had the freedom either to accept or to reject the proffered gift. And the gesture appeared quite pointless, for there was an ample supply of fig-leaves in the vicinity.

The first reference to a sacrifice offered by man is found in Genesis 4:3–5. Both Cain and Abel offered gifts to God, but God looked favourably only on Abel's sacrifice. Hebrews 11:4 comments, 'It was because of his faith that Abel offered God a better sacrifice than Cain, and for that he was declared to be righteous when God made acknowledgement of his offerings.' Cain only gave God 'some of the produce of the soil', whereas Abel sacrificed 'the first-born of his flock and some of their fat as well'.

Nothing in the context suggests that these early sacrifices were made to earn God's favour; it seems that they were a natural attempt to express human thanks. Both gifts were offered to God, and he accepted one and rejected the other. God did not need what either man offered; but he deserved the best, and Abel's offering was better, bloodier, and costlier than his brother's. So God preferred the younger to the elder, something he was to do time and again throughout the Bible, showing his freedom of choice, his contempt for earthly standards of prominence, and his regard for the lowly.

Noah made the next recorded sacrifice. In Genesis 8:20 we read that after the Flood had subsided Noah built the first altar and offered God a burnt-offering of clean birds and beasts in thanks for his family's safe deliverance. It appears to have been a spontaneous gesture of praise and commitment, as God had neither requested thanks, nor needed what was offered. But God was so pleased with Noah's sacrifice that he rewarded him, in 8:21—9:17, with the promise of glorious future blessing.

Abraham must have been in the habit of offering God sacrifices from his flocks of sheep, or Isaac would not have asked about the lamb (Genesis 22:7). In that chapter God asked man for a sacrifice for the first time; and he wanted the best. Abraham was ordered to offer Isaac as a burnt-offering on Mount Moriah—the place where the Jerusalem Temple would eventually be sited. Isaac, who by then was aged about thirty, was prepared to be the willing victim; and his elderly father was ready to sacrifice his only son. But how pointless must the proposed death have appeared to both of them, especially after all God's promises through the years!

Faith and sacrifice were first linked with reference to Abel, and by faith Abraham seized the knife and prepared to plunge it into his son. Human reasoning usually concludes that sacrifice seems stupid; however Abraham believed that God knew best. He did not understand why God wanted him to kill his son. He did not know that nearly two thousand years later God would go through similar but stronger agonies on exactly the same mountain. Abraham simply acted with faith and prepared to obey his God.

In verse 5 Abraham told his two servants that he and Isaac were going to worship. At first sight this seems a remarkably inappropriate description for the intended act of killing one's only son. But the Hebrew word for worship, *shachah*, means to bow the self down, to sink down. Many today mistakenly understand worship to mean singing songs, saying prayers, listening to sermons, and, maybe, enjoying spiritual gifts. But these activities can only be called worship if self is bowed down. God is worshipped whenever a man's self is truly bowed before God in recognition that his will is best and should be accepted with thanksgiving. What God does must be right, regardless of whether or not it makes any human sense. His will may mean waiting, failing, suffering, even dying, and when these are willingly embraced as part of his mysterious purpose God is always worshipped. Abraham put aside his plans for Isaac, his reputation with his servants, his love for his wife, and bowed his self to God's will. When he raised the knife he reached heights of worship unknown to most today who regularly raise their arms in praise and prayer.

God responded to Abraham's faith-filled willingness to sacrifice his only son with the promise, in verses 15–18, of enormous blessing. Abraham and Isaac had been ready for death without any hint of reward. They just wanted to please God, and they knew he was pleased by sacrifice. Faith-filled, selfless, loving obedience was their sole motivation. But once again God's grace rewarded man's sacrifice with a glorious promise of future blessing. This link between blessing and sacrifice is repeated in Genesis 46:1–4 where Jacob's sacrifice at Beersheba was followed by the twin promises of God's presence and future reward.

The Egyptians endured the ten plagues because Pharaoh would not allow the Israelites to spend three days in the wilderness worshipping God through sacrifice. Exodus 5:1–5 introduces the saga which fills nine chapters, and before each plague Yahweh's message to Pharaoh was, 'Let my people go to offer me worship.'

Exodus 10:24–26 highlights two important aspects of sacrifice. Firstly, wild animals were unacceptable, only clean animals and birds which belonged to the one making the sacrifice could be offered. The people themselves could eat any available clean wild beasts and birds, but their sacrifices for God had to deplete their personal resources: there had to be a real element of self-denial for the sacrifice to have any meaning. And, secondly, because they wanted to please God they realised that they should allow him to direct their sacrifices. Moses told Pharaoh, 'Until we reach the place, we do not know ourselves what worship we shall have to offer Yahweh' (10:26).

The tenth plague introduced two new strands into the Old Testament story of sacrifice. Exodus 12 supplies the details of the Passover: firstly, the people were now to offer a sacrifice with a personal benefit in mind; and, secondly, they were to go on offering an identical annual sacrifice as a ritualistic act of thanksgiving and remembrance. The initiative was all God's. The provision of the Passover sacrifice was the evidence both of God's love for his people and of his grace. Each family had personally to appropriate God's provision: the sacrifice of their best animal, and the sprinkling of its blood on the doorposts and lintel was their faith-filled response to God's grace. And once again God rewarded his people's obedient sacrifices with blessing, this time with a personal deliverance from death and a national deliverance from slavery, in a display of sheer power which revealed his great glory.

In the wilderness God gave the Israelites clear instructions about sacrifice. Brief outlines can be read in Exodus 20:24–26; 22:29–30; 23:14–19; 29; Leviticus 17; 23; Numbers 15; and Deuteronomy 12 and 16. A fuller description in Leviticus 1–7 outlines the five principal rituals: the holocaust, or wholly-burnt offering; the oblation, or cereal offering; the communion, or peace offering; the sin offering; and the reparation, or guilt offering.

In all these sacrifices only the best material would do

for God. We have already noted that the worshipper had to sacrifice in a way that seriously depleted his personal resources, but Deuteronomy 23:18 suggests that even this would be unacceptable if the property had been unlawfully acquired. Male animals were preferred to females, and the mature first-born was especially favoured. They had to be perfect specimens: the animal chosen for sacrifice was always the one that would have most improved the owner's stock. God's justice meant that the poor were not penalised by these demands: Leviticus 5:7–13 shows that those who were unable to afford a sheep or goat could offer two doves or two pigeons, and if they could not afford this, then an oblation would suffice instead.

The sacrifices were to be offered personally and nationally, privately and publicly, regularly and as special needs arose. Numbers 28 and 29 give a full list of the daily, weekly, monthly and annual public sacrifices, and Exodus 12 shows how the Passover was to be celebrated privately within the family unit. Sacrifices were offered to fulfil a vow, 2 Samuel 15:7–9, and to release a man from a vow, Numbers 6; as a spontaneous act of worship, Judges 13:17–23; at the purification both of a woman after childbirth, and of a leper, Leviticus 12 and 14; at the ordination of a priest, and at the offering of a Levite to God, Leviticus 8 and Numbers 8; at times of national repentance, 1 Samuel 7, and at an impending battle, 1 Samuel 13:8–12; at royal coronations, 1 Kings 1:9, 11–12, and at the dedication of sanctuaries, 1 Kings 8:1–13. Whatever the reason, whenever the people turned to God they worshipped him by offering him sacrifices.

The Old Testament ritual sacrifices had six stages, and

each one was as significant as the other five. First, the worshipper selected or purchased his sacrifice and brought it to the designated place. If the offering was an animal he then placed his hand on it to show that it was his representative or substitute; and if it was a sin or guilt offering he also confessed his sins to transfer them symbolically to the sacrifice. Thirdly, the worshipper personally killed the animal. Next, the priests collected the blood in a basin and poured it against two opposite corners of the altar so that all four sides were splashed. Fifthly, the fat was burnt, and, with a holocaust, everything else was also burnt except for the skin. And, lastly, what remained of the sacrifice was eaten by the priests; if it was a communion sacrifice the remainder was eaten by the priests and worshippers together.

The holocaust and the communion sacrifice were used for all the purposes mentioned earlier, but particularly for celebration and thanksgiving, the consecration of persons and things for holy service, and for the removal of ceremonial uncleanness. However, the other sacrifices had a deeper purpose: Leviticus repeatedly states that a man's sin offering or guilt offering would 'be accepted as effectual for his atonement'. The Hebrew verb *capar*, 'to atone', means to cover, and these sacrifices covered up the worshipper's sin and cancelled his guilt. Just as the first sacrifice was offered by God's blood-stained hands as a makeshift cover for Adam and Eve's sorry sinful state, so God now provided his people with a series of sacrifices which could go on temporarily covering up their sin, guilt and shame.

The holocaust and communion sacrifices helped the people express their feelings of being creatures who belonged by right to God. The 'wholly-burned' holocaust represented the dedication by man, and acceptance by God, of everything that the worshipper had and was; and the eating together by priest and man of the communion reminded them of the vital relationship between creature and Creator. The sin and guilt sacrifices enabled the people to display their human sense of separation from a holy God caused by their sin and guilt, and to cry to him for it to be covered. But despite these important distinctions all the legal sacrifices stressed God's gracious initiative and the people's absolute dependence upon him.

As time went by the ritualistic system of sacrifice was abused, and the realisation grew that the system was not final. God's prophets began to plead for an extra type of sacrifice, for practical actions as well as, not instead of, symbolic gestures; for personal morality to be wedded to legal ritual. Psalm 50:8–23; 51:16–19; Proverbs 15:8; 21:27; Isaiah 58:1–14; 66:1–4, 18–21; Jeremiah 6:20; 7:21–28; Daniel 3:38–43; Hosea 8:11–13; Amos 5:21–24; and Micah 6:6–8 all illustrate this critical development in the prophetic awareness of God's desires, but nowhere is this expressed more clearly than in Isaiah 1:11–20. 'What are your endless sacrifices to me? says Yahweh. I am sick of holocausts of rams and the fat of calves. The blood of bulls and of goats revolts me… Bring me your worthless offerings no more, the smoke of them fills me with disgust…Cease to do evil. Learn to do good, search for justice, help the oppressed, be just to the orphan, plead for the widow.'

This new understanding of sacrifice as both a ceremony for personal atonement and also a continuous holy way of life reached its Old Testament climax in the four songs of the servant of Yahweh recorded in Isaiah 42:1–9;

49:1–6; 50:4–11; and 52:13–53:12. These songs present a person whose death makes sacrificial atonement for others and whose life is characterised by love, justice, humility, suffering and sacrifice.

The first three songs show that this mysterious servant is an individual formed by Yahweh and called by him while still in his mother's womb. He is a disciple who is filled with God's Spirit. He establishes justice on earth so that he may instruct mankind and judge them by his word. He works gently, quietly and discreetly. He appears to fail, accepts outrage and contempt, but does not give up because Yahweh himself sustains him.

The fourth song describes the appalling sufferings of the servant who, though innocent, is treated as a sinner punished by God and condemned to die a shameful death. It shows that all this is the servant's voluntary offering for sinners whose sin and guilt he takes on to himself and for whom he intercedes. And the song reveals that, by a previously unimaginable act of power, God accepts the atoning sacrifice of his servant and brings about the salvation of all men.

These extraordinary prophetic songs point to Jesus. In fact, all the Old Testament sacrifices point in some way to him, for they express a need which only he fully satisfies, and embody a faith which he alone can justify. But more than that they demand a lifestyle which only he makes possible. The victim slain may have been a substitute, but the worshipper always had to deny himself in some way for God. And these two principles need to be remembered today. Christ may have died in our place permanently to cover our sin, unite us with each other, and bring us to God, but self-denial is still the 'ritual' demanded of the lives that he rules.

The
Sacrificial
Life of Christ

Suffering and rejection are laid upon Jesus as a divine necessity, and every attempt to prevent it is the work of the devil.

Dietrich Bonhoeffer

Glory and sacrifice are central to the life of Jesus. From before the beginning he was with God and he was God. He was all-powerful, all-seeing, all-knowing, all-loving, and everywhere at the same time. He dwelt in perpetual glory and was himself all-glorious. Glory was his nature and his surroundings; in fact glory was the sum total of Jesus' eternal experience. And this visible glory was what he offered as his first sacrifice.

The Father did not make the Son surrender his glory: he relinquished it quite willingly. Jesus' state was divine, yet he did not cling to his equality with God but instead emptied himself. He shed every attribute which expresses and reveals the essential nature of God. He laid aside his majesty and picked up the mantle of humanity. He put down his omnipotence, his omnipresence and his omniscience, and put on all the weaknesses of men except sin. He stepped out of the glory to which he was entitled and, therefore, stopped looking like God. He did not cease to be God, because he could not give up his divine nature; instead he sacrificed the public treatment and honour due to him because he was God, assumed the condition of a human slave, and made himself nothing.

The Word through whom all things came into being voluntarily became a precarious foetus in a teenage womb. One moment he was the great God surrounded by limitless glory, the next he was a mass of cells suspended in a woman's body. One minute he had been the very Wisdom of God, the next he had neither memory nor intellect, not even the power to pray. Christ's sacrifice meant that he could not talk, could not walk, and could not control his bladder.

He was oblivious of the degradation at his birth. He was unaware of the shepherds' homage or the astrologers' gifts. He knew nothing of his parents' frantic flight to Egypt because of Herod's threats to his small life. His earliest earthly experiences were the shame of illegitimacy, the bewilderment of refugees, the oppression of an occupying power, and then the unique emotional strain of a growing appreciation of his divine nature and mission. Yet this was the way of life he had freely chosen, for Jesus had deliberately sacrificed his glory to embrace the filth of humanity. And he has called us to follow him.

We do not know when Jesus first became aware of his divine nature and messianic calling, though certainly he had some idea when he was twelve. But he remained silent, quietly obeying his parents. He learned to work with his hands, he wept when Joseph died, and waited for his mission to begin. Nobody thought he was different or special, he was just another irrelevant manual worker in a remote part of the Roman empire. But he was God. He could have arranged things differently. He could have been reared in an emperor's palace. He could have continuously radiated the obvious glory of God. He could even have resuscitated Joseph. But by a deliberate act of self-sacrifice he chose to personify a holy contentment with human poverty, obscurity, and indifference.

When Jesus finally began his mission he gave up the

relative comforts of his Nazareth home, the financial security of his carpentry business, and the understanding and support of his younger brothers. His cousin was calling sinners to repent and to show this by being baptised. So Jesus joined the queue. He didn't ask John to step aside and let him take over. He didn't whisper to the next man that, actually, he was faultless and didn't need to be baptised. Instead he stood where sinners stood and endured the speculating glances of people who wondered what it was the carpenter had done that was so wrong. And when his cousin protested, Jesus' only comment was, 'Leave it like this for the time being; it is fitting that we should, in this way, do all that righteousness demands' (Matthew 3:15). The Father reacted to this sacrifice as he had to so many before, with the gift of a glimpse of glory, the sign of his permanent presence, and the promise of his divine favour. 'The heavens opened and he saw the Spirit of God descending like a dove and coming down on him. And a voice spoke from heaven, "This is my Son, the Beloved; my favour rests on him."'

Self-sacrifice dominated Jesus' ministry. He spent six weeks in the wilderness without food, resisting temptations unequalled in strength throughout history. He had nowhere to lay his head at night. He healed with no expectation of any gratitude. He taught without claiming any earthly reward. He entrusted what little money he had to a man who misappropriated it. He befriended prostitutes, alcoholics, terrorists, the terminally ill, and those who were financially corrupt. He embraced lepers —the first century equivalent of kissing a bleeding AIDS sufferer. He frequently asserted that he could do nothing by himself. He washed feet, went without sleep, and was usually misunderstood. Without any doubt he was

Isaiah's suffering servant. True, Pilate recognised that Jesus was the real King of the Jews. Certainly a few of his close friends realised he was the Son of God. Undoubtably most people thought he was a very good man. But he was not the kind of King or God or Perfect Man that people either expected or wanted.

They longed for another king like David who would establish a powerful independent kingdom; but though Jesus was the Son of David he would not rule in the same way as David. The people wanted a God like the one who had led them in power out of Egypt and had kept on showing them his glory in an obvious way; but though Jesus was the Son of God he would not awe them with a blaze of glory. They hoped for a Perfect Man like the one promised in Daniel 7:13–14 who would be served by men of all peoples, nations and languages; but even though Jesus was that Son of Man he had come to serve not to be served, and to ask men to serve others with him, not just to serve him with others. Jesus' life was full of obvious self-sacrifice and, because of this, he was rejected. The people did not want his type of Messiah.

Suffering can be heroic. A suffering king can be honoured and respected. A suffering man can earn sympathy and applause. A suffering God may still be worthy of worship. And if Jesus had simply endured suffering he might have been universally admired. But Jesus also sacrificed admiration and acceptance, choosing to be despised and rejected; and it is this rejection which robs his suffering of human honour.

As soon as the disciples realised that he was the Christ, Jesus explained to them what this meant: 'And he began to teach them that the Son of Man was destined to suffer grievously, to be rejected by the elders and the chief priests and the scribes, and to be put to death, and after three days to rise again.' (Matthew 16:21; Mark 8:31–32; Luke 9:22.) This was anathema to the disciples, so Peter took Jesus aside to remonstrate with him. Peter did not want to follow a suffering Christ; the disciples did not want a Lord who would be rejected. They neither understood nor believed that God's way for his Beloved could mean suffering, rejection, death, and then resurrection. But Jesus rebuked them, said that their well-meaning protests were evil in origin, and told them that the divine demand for self-sacrifice applied to them as well as him. He said, in Matthew 16:24 and Mark 8:34, 'If anyone wants to be a follower of mine, let him renounce himself and take up his cross and follow me.' Luke 9:23 adds that this must be done 'every day'.

These words were spoken to those who had already begun to follow Jesus, to those who had already seen God work signs and wonders through their hands, to those who had sampled the simple lifestyle demanded in Luke 9:1–6, and to those who had just realised that the one they were following was heading straight for rejection and sacrifice. Now that they knew the truth, Jesus set them free to choose self or to choose self-sacrifice. He expected nothing of them, demanded nothing from them, and forced nothing upon them; he simply offered his own example and exposed himself to yet more rejection.

To follow Christ is to say 'death to self'. This is not a series of occasional ascetic gestures, nor is it suicide, for that is self-indulgent. Instead it means I must be unaware of my self and aware only of Christ; that I must have my eyes so fixed on the one I am following that I am blind to the path which is too steep for me, and deaf to the blisters which plead with me to stop; that I must know that nothing in this life can compare to the glory waiting for me, if I have stuck close to his bent and beaten back.

When I follow Christ I must show that I mean death to my self by taking up my God-offered cross. This will not be an ailment or difficulty indistinguishable from those endured by all men, but some form of suffering and rejection for the sake of Christ which is reserved for those who follow him. Everyone who aspires to be his follower will have already been allocated a share of suffering and rejection. Each person who responds to Christ's call to walk in his footsteps has his own personal cross awaiting collection. Each follower is meant to consider himself to have the same short life-expectancy as those who rot on every Death Row all round the world. This self-death is not a calamity, but the fruit of commitment; it is not a sad accident, but a spiritual appointment; and it is not the end of everything, but rather the beginning of abundant life with Christ.

The twelve heard these new requirements of discipleship in silence, and nobody walked away. So, perhaps predictably, Jesus offered them, in Matthew 16:27 and Luke 9:26, a hint of future glory. And within a few days, at the Transfiguration, God dramatically underlined both this hint and the importance of Jesus' words. It should not now surprise any reader that the only moment during Jesus' earthly life when he was seen surrounded by visible glory followed his first mention of his passion. God's words show how pleased he was by Christ's announcement of his own impending sacrifice, and the importance of Christ's demands on his followers: 'This is my Son, the Beloved; he enjoys my favour. *Listen to him*.'

As the time of Jesus' ultimate sacrifice drew near he

began to teach more clearly about self-sacrifice. He told his followers that if they wanted to be great they must not make their authority felt or lord it over people, but rather be the servants and slaves of all (Matthew 20:25–27; Mark 10:41–45; and Luke 22:24–27). He entered Jerusalem seated on a humble donkey to demonstrate the unpretentious peaceful nature of his rule (Matthew 21:1–11; Mark 11:1–11; Luke 19:28–38; and John 12:12–16). He agreed that it was far more important for a man to love God with all his heart, understanding and strength, and to love his neighbour as himself, than to offer holocausts (Mark 12:28–34). He commended the widow who discreetly donated everything she possessed (Mark 12:41–44). He stated that Mary's extravagant anointing of him with a pound of pure nard worth a working man's annual wage was not a waste but a good work worth remembering and retelling in the context of the good news (Matthew 26:6–13; Mark 14:3–9; John 12:1–8). He washed his disciples' feet to show the perfection of his love and to provide an example for them to follow (John 13:1–16). And, perhaps most important of all, he taught Philip and Andrew the principle that self-sacrifice is the secret of fruitfulness.

This principle is written deep across God's creation: before any seed can multiply it must die and cease to be. If the seed seeks to preserve its own independent existence it remains a single grain, but if it dies and disappears it yields a rich harvest. In John 12:23–33 Jesus took this principle and applied it to himself, but he was not only thinking of himself for, in verses 25 and 26, he expressly applied the same principle to all who would follow him. These words once again link glory with sacrifice: Jesus has freely offered his death so he knows that he can ask for the Father's name to be glorified, and the Father's audible reply emphasised his presence and again promised the reward of future glory.

Truly Jesus was the suffering servant first introduced by Isaiah. He did not shout or raise his voice. He was gentle with the weak, but utterly just. He gave sight to the blind and liberated prisoners, but exhausted himself and appeared to work in vain. He was courageous, patient, pure, and meek. He was only honoured by God, his only reward was with God, and God was his only source of strength and speech. Although his back was beaten, his beard plucked, and his face spat upon, he set his face like flint and persevered with his arduous task. He was despised and rejected, a man of sorrows familiar with suffering. He was punished, struck, pierced, wounded, burdened, and crushed with suffering by Yahweh. And this suffering, self-sacrificing servant is the one who has called us to follow him.

The Sacrificial Death of Christ

"There cannot be a God of love," men say, "because if there was, and he looked upon the world, his heart would break." The Church points to the Cross and says, "It did break."

William Temple

Judas Iscariot believed that Jesus died because he had betrayed him to his enemies. Caiaphas and the other Jewish leaders were convinced that Jesus had died because they had demanded his death. The people presumed that Jesus' death was due to their pleas for Barabbas' release. Pontius Pilate thought Jesus had died because he had sentenced him to be killed by crucifixion. And if anyone had asked the Roman soldiers they would have said it was all down to their skills as public executioners. They were all right. They had killed Jesus. But they were also all wrong, because the language of sacrifice is inseparable from the story of the cross.

At his baptism Jesus stood with other sinners. During his temptations he refused the easy path to fame and worship. And throughout his life he repeatedly predicted his death (Matthew 20:28; 26:1–2, 24; Mark 14:21; Luke 13:31–33; John 2:19–22; 6:48–58; 7:2–8, 19, 33; 12:7, 23–34; 15:13). He made it clear that he had to be lifted up like Moses' serpent in the wilderness (John 3:13–14; 8:28). Three times he prophesied about his passion (Matthew 16:21–23; 17:22–23; 20:17–19; Mark 8:31–33; 9:30–32; 10:32–34; Luke 9:22, 44–45). He announced that he was the Good Shepherd who would lay down his life for his sheep of his own free will (John

10:11–18). He deliberately walked to Jerusalem proclaiming that he would be handed over to the priests, condemned to death, then passed to the pagans to be mocked, scourged and crucified (Luke 18:31–34). By publicly relating a parable about some wicked husbandmen he showed his opponents that he knew their plans (Matthew 21:33–43; Mark 12:1–11; Luke 20:9–18). At the Last Supper he told his disciples that his body and blood would be given for them, not taken from him (Luke 22:15–22). And throughout the New Testament Christ's death is recognised as essentially sacrificial (1 Corinthians 5:7; 2 Corinthians 5:14; Galatians 2:20; Ephesians 5:2; Hebrews 5–10; 1 Peter 3:18; and 1 John 2:2).

The four servant songs of Isaiah describe not only the sacrificial life of Jesus, Yahweh's servant, but also his sacrificial death. In particular, the fourth song is remarkable for its detailed predictions about the physical agonies and spiritual consequences of that death; only Psalm 22 approaches Isaiah 53 for prophetic accuracy about Christ's passion. However, in this study I am not primarily concerned with either the agonies or the consequences of his death, but with what it teaches about sacrifice.

We know that Jesus endured unimaginable physical, emotional and spiritual torments. We know that he died once and for all for us and for our sins to bring us to God. We know that his death appeased God's anger, satisfied God's sense of justice, earned our forgiveness, purchased our freedom, declared our righteousness, and forged our new relationships with God and man. We know that his sacrifice has achieved the eternal perfection of all whom he is sanctifying. And we know that his single sacrifice for sin has fully atoned for all sins so that there is now no need for sin and guilt offerings.

But there is more to Christ's death even than all this. Undoubtedly, we personally need to know, appreciate, and appropriate all the benefits of his death; but we also need to recognise that, as well as ending the need for substitutionary sacrifices, his death also provided the supreme example of self-sacrifice which all his disciples are expected to follow: 1 Peter 2:21–25 argues this most forcibly.

The fourth servant song contains a phrase which is difficult to translate, but which is important for our study on sacrifice. The second clause of Isaiah 53:10 could mean 'though God offers his servant as a guilt offering' or 'though the servant offers himself as a guilt offering': it is unclear from the Hebrew whether it is God or the servant who makes the offering. At first sight the New Testament appears to be equally ambiguous on this point.

Perhaps the most famous verse in the Bible is John 3:16, and this tells us that it was God who gave his Son. Jesus' parable of the wicked husbandmen affirms that it was the owner who decided to send his beloved son to be killed by the tenants. Mark 14:27; Romans 3:25; 4:25; 8:3, 32; and 2 Corinthians 5:21 all further underline that the Father sacrificed his only Son. 1 John 4:9–10 expresses this very clearly, 'God sent into the world his only Son so that we could have life through him...he sent his Son to be the sacrifice that takes our sins away.'

Yet elsewhere in the New Testament the voluntary nature of Christ's sacrifice is stressed. Jesus himself said, in Matthew 20:28, that he had come to give his life. Galatians 2:20; Ephesians 5:25; 1 Timothy 2:6; Titus 2:14 and Hebrews 9:26 all affirm that the Son sacrificed himself. Ephesians 5:2 states that he gave himself up as a fragrant offering and sacrifice. And Hebrews 9:14 says that he offered himself as the perfect sacrifice to God.

The truth is, of course, double-sided. The Father gave the Son, and the Son freely gave himself. The Father sacrificed his only Son, and the Son voluntarily sacrificed himself. The Father did not make the Son endure an ordeal he was unwilling to bear, and the Son did not surprise his Father by his selfless action. Galatians 1:4 neatly expresses this paradox by asserting that Jesus 'sacrificed himself for our sins, in accordance with the will of God our Father'. And Jesus himself put the matter quite plainly in John 10:17–18, 'The Father loves me, because I lay down my life in order to take it up again. No one takes it from me; I lay it down of my own free will, and as it is in my power to lay it down, so it is in my power to take it up again; and this is the command I have been given by my Father.'

In one sense the story of Abraham and Isaac on Mount Moriah is an obvious precedent, for there we see the father ready to sacrifice his favourite son, and that same son prepared to be the willing victim. But at another level it is a thoroughly inadequate picture because it reveals nothing at all of God's essential oneness.

We saw in Book two of this trilogy that God is not divided into three. He is one, but more than one. The Father, the Son and the Spirit are not three distinct individuals but three self-distinctions within one being, who reveal their oneness in a threefold diversity of persons, characteristics and functions. And if this divine unity is misunderstood we are likely to fall into a dangerous error whenever we gaze at the cross. For if we think of the Father, the Son and the Spirit as separate individuals we inevitably caricature Calvary as either God punishing an innocent Son or as Jesus persuading a reluctant Father. But Paul makes it clear in 2 Corinthians 5:18–19 that our sacrifice was not made by Christ alone or by God alone, but by God acting in and through Christ with his full agreement. They worked together in harmony. Their wills were one. They would not be separated.

The essential unity of God could lead us to conclude that God died for us. After all, 1 Corinthians 2:8 shows that it was the Lord of Glory who was crucified; the Lamb who died is seen throughout Revelation to be at the very centre of God's throne; and Hebrews 9:17 argues that we can only benefit from the promises in a will after the testator has died. But because God is immortal he could not have died. To solve this problem God became man so that he could die in our place; so that he could both inflict and receive his own punishment; and so that he could simultaneously be both Judge and innocent victim: Hebrews 2:14–18 and Philippians 2:6–8 state this clearly.

This means that we must worship God as a God of sacrifice, and that we must consider sacrifice as not only central to Scripture but as also the very heart of God's nature. His sacrifice on the cross eternally achieved our salvation and finally disclosed his character; but the great glory of the cross is not our salvation but his self-disclosure. We saw in chapter one that glory is the word used to describe the self-revelation of God's character. And we saw in chapter two that God's glory is seen only at a place of sacrifice. Therefore it should not surprise us that God's own supreme sacrifice is the place where his glory shines most brightly.

'Glory' must be the only appropriate description of the cross as the cross unveils, more clearly than anything else in history, what God is really like, and it decisively shows his active presence in the world. So when we cry 'glory' today we should remember the cross. Jesus did. John 12:20–32; 13:30–32; and 17:1–5 show the link in Jesus' mind between glory and the cross, and the fact that the glory is a glorification of both Father and Son together: it is the one God who is glorified on the cross.

The shining glory of the cross is the supreme revelation by his sacrifice of God's goodness, God's mercy, God's grace, God's truth, God's patience, God's forgiveness, God's righteousness, God's peace, God's self-control, God's gentleness, God's self-effacement, God's trustfulness, God's faith; but, above all these, of God's justice, and, above everything, God's love. Romans 3:24–26 says, '…Jesus was appointed by God to sacrifice his life so as to win reconciliation through faith. In this way God makes his justice known; first, for the past, when sins went unpunished because he held his hand, then, for the present age, by showing positively that he is just and that he justifies everyone who believes in Jesus.' And Romans 5:8 states simply, 'But what proves that God loves us is that Christ died for us while we were still sinners.'

Until the cross God's justice had not been startlingly obvious on earth. Sinners had prospered and evil had gone unpunished, so God had appeared to be impotent, unjust, and morally indifferent. But his long-suffering had been a postponement of judgement, not a cancellation. At the cross God, by his sacrifice, finally revealed his just nature by condemning all sins in Christ, and on the cross he gave a visible proof of his justice by himself bearing, in Christ, his just punishment for all the evil in the world. Since the sacrifice on the cross God can no longer be accused of condoning evil or of being unjust, because his justice in judging and punishing sin has, once and for all, been clearly and convincingly shown.

Until the cross God's love had not been especially apparent to mankind. Disease, disasters, decay, even death, all argued against God being characterised by love. Tragedy, torture, tyranny and tribulation all seemed irreconcilable with a God of love. But at the cross God, by his sacrifice, partially unveiled his immeasurable, inexhaustible, unknowable, self-giving love. The writers of the New Testament always define love in terms of God's sacrifice on the cross: for example, Romans 5:8; 1 John 3:15–20; and 4:7–21. At the cross the Son died, stretched by soldiers between two thieves and the Father left him alone. Why? Because of their love for the thieves, the torturers, and all those who had pleaded for his death. At the cross God gave everything because of his love for those who deserve nothing. The Father gave his Son for those who prefer to worship other gods. The Son gave himself for those who steadfastly ignore him. And they both surrendered their relationship with each other because of their unimaginable love for you and me. Since the dreadful agony and divine separation of the sacrifice at Calvary no man can look at a cross and question God's love, because nothing could demonstrate God's love more clearly than this total self-sacrifice.

The sacrificial death of Jesus took place because of God's justice and love: there was no other motivation. Jesus' death had many consequences, but amongst them was this perfect revelation of God's love and justice, and the provision of the perfect example for all Jesus' disciples to follow. So it surely follows that those who do tread in his footsteps should carefully and prayerfully ensure that all their sacrifices are also motivated only by God's justice and love. And if this is so they can be confident of two things: firstly, that their sacrifice will reveal to men something of God's character and presence in a way that nothing else can; and secondly, that the God of sacrifice will himself share in their agony, isolation and deprivation. And in both of these consequences there is glory.

Sacrifice in the Early Church

The world says power and position are synonymous and that the goal of power is control. Jesus says the goal of the Christian is to serve others and glorify God, and the way to such service is through the cross. This is true power, however foolish it appears to the world.

Howard Snyder

The first Christians knew that the Old Testament prophets had pleaded with Israel to offer God sacrifice through practical actions like helping the oppressed, caring for widows, giving justice to orphans, and providing for the poor. The first Christians had also heard Jesus teach that his final judgement of them would hinge on the degree to which they had fed the hungry, satisfied the thirsty, welcomed strangers, clothed the naked, and visited those who were ill or in prison. So, naturally, these were the sort of sacrifices which dominated their lives.

The members of the early church did not merely give to the poor and feel sorry for the needy, for that would only have been concerned paternalism and not Christian sacrifice. Compassionate, charitable giving which does not noticeably alter individual or collective lifestyles has always been the predictable pagan response to human need; but allegiance to Christ should result in individual and congregational lifestyles which go on being visibly and dramatically transformed by Christ's sacrificial life and death. Such results are clearly seen in the three descriptions of the earliest Christian way of life in Acts 2:44–47; 4:32–35; and 5:12–16.

God's love motivated the first Christians to sacrifice

their independent attitudes, their possessions and their financial resources. Their awareness of God's justice meant that the wealthy few could not live in comfort while many of their brothers and sisters went without. And the pattern of God's oneness ensured that the several thousand Christian men and women in one town managed to live harmoniously together. They owned everything in common. They sold their goods and possessions, dividing the proceeds among themselves according to what each one needed. They shared their food gladly and generously. No one claimed for his own use anything that he had. And consequently nobody was ever in want, as the wealthiest sold their assets and presented the proceeds to the leaders who redistributed the money to those in need.

Acts 6:1–2 shows that the financial sacrifices were extensive enough to enable the first believers to organise and maintain a daily food distribution to the needy. When this ran into difficulties seven Spirit-filled men with good reputations and obvious wisdom were set apart to oversee the task. That seven men were needed shows the size of the job, and the qualities demanded of them indicates the importance credited to their function. I wonder how many deacons are appointed by congregations to perform a similar job today.

In order to have any integrity the leaders of the early church must surely have set the foremost example of financial sacrifice. Certainly Acts 3:1–10 tells us that Peter and John had no money on them when they were accosted by a lame middle-aged beggar. Would the man have been healed if Peter or John still had some money? I doubt it. It may be impossible to prove a causal link, but it is worth noting that mighty miracles and astonishing numerical growth coincided with the early church's extravagant financial sacrifices. Perhaps the blessing was a foreshadowing of the heavenly glory due to them as the eternal reward for their earthly sacrifices.

Barnabas, a Levite from Cyprus, owned a piece of land. He sold it, and gave all the proceeds to the apostles for redistribution among the needy. This action, mentioned in Acts 4:37, surely merits the label 'sacrifice', for Barnabas sacrificed his capital instead of giving from his income. Never again could he use his piece of land, call it his own, or let it and live off the rent. But I think that the most important element in this sacrifice is Barnabas' relinquishment of control. For so many today the most enjoyable elements of giving are the selection of the charitable cause and the evaluation of the amount to be given. But Barnabas not only permanently sacrificed all his land, he also refused to exercise any control over the distribution of the proceeds. He neither personally picked the individual beneficiaries nor weighed up what he could afford to give. Instead he sold his land, and let others choose who would benefit from his sacrifice. Many today would condemn Barnabas as rash and financially irresponsible, but I think God caused his generosity to be recorded in Acts as a sacrifice to be imitated rather than an action to be avoided.

Agabus predicted a famine, Acts 11:27–30, so the Antioch disciples all contributed what they could afford for the support of their Judean brothers. Today God doesn't waste his prophets' words with warnings of forthcoming famines. Why? Because we don't even respond sacrificially to live television pictures of our starving African brothers dying in present-day famines.

In Philippians 4:10–20 Paul suggests that the financial

sacrifices made by the Philippian believers meant that they had shared his hardships. Not only had the Philippians' generosity helped ease Paul's financial shortage, but it had caused them to become as needy as he had been! Their extravagant giving resulted in Paul having more than he needed and in the Philippian believers becoming so needy that only God could fulfil their needs. That's sacrifice! When will our giving show we so love our third world brothers and sisters that we are willing to share their hardships? When will we sacrifice financially to such an extent that, even if only temporarily, they have more than they need and we become needier than they were?

Peter, Paul, and whoever wrote Hebrews unite in expecting Christ's followers to go on making sacrifices. Hebrews is a long letter about sacrifice which is mostly taken up with proving that Christ's death was the once-and-for-all atoning sacrifice for sin. However, the writer of Hebrews concludes his epistle with a plea, in 13:13–16, for his readers both to share in Christ's degradation and also to offer God an unending sacrifice. He suggests that this sacrifice has the three aspects of unceasing praise to God, frequent good works, and the continual sharing of personal resources.

1 Peter 2:4–5 is the most well-known New Testament passage about sacrifices: 'He is the living stone, rejected by men but chosen by God and precious to him; set yourselves close to him so that you too, the holy priesthood that offers the spiritual sacrifices which Jesus Christ has made acceptable to God, may be living stones making a spiritual house.' Peter wrote these words from Rome at the outbreak of Nero's horrific persecutions of the church. His own death was imminent, and it seemed

likely that believers throughout the rest of the Empire would soon be suffering in a similar way to those in Rome. Against this backdrop the word 'sacrifice' resonates with its original bloody and terminal meaning. In such circumstances Peter's use of the word sacrifice must deliberately infer a permanent loss, a costly self-denial, and the imitation of Christ's death.

In Romans 12:1 Paul explicitly pleads for sacrifice: 'Think of God's mercy, my brothers, and worship him, I beg you, in a way that is worthy of thinking beings, by offering your living bodies as a holy sacrifice, truly pleasing to God'; and in Ephesians 5:1–2 he implicitly asks for sacrifice when he writes, 'Try, then, to imitate God, as children of his that he loves, and follow Christ by loving as he loved you, giving himself up in our place as a fragrant offering and a sacrifice to God.'

Interestingly, both Paul and Peter develop their demands for sacrifice in a very similar way to the writer of Hebrews. Compare the three aspects of sacrifice listed in Hebrews 13:15–16 with Peter's statement in 1 Peter 2:9 that the royal priesthood is set apart 'to sing the praises of God', and his words in 2:11–3:17 where he lists the attitudes and obligations of Christians towards bigoted pagans, evil civil authorities, unconverted spouses, unfair employers, and each other. Peter justifies these demands by constant reference to Christ as the Servant of Isaiah's fourth servant song who suffered in silence.

In Romans 12:2–15:13 Paul urges his readers towards humility, interdependence, unpretentious love, hard work, cheerfulness, perseverance, submission to both civil authorities and the whims of the scrupulous, charity for enemies, oneness with each other, and sacrificial generosity, 'If any of the saints are in need you *must* share with them' (12:13). In Ephesians 5:1—6:9 he emphasises the need for pure speech, praise and thanksgiving; and, like Peter, he lists the attitudes and obligations of Christians towards spouses, employers, and employees.

These three passages suggest that the early church did not understand the phrase 'spiritual sacrifice' to be an all-embracing expression for any act of a spirit-filled man, but to mean something quite specific. It seems to me that the early church leaders taught God's people to make one sacrifice which, like the ritual sacrifice of the Old Testament, had several distinctive elements, each element being as significant as the others. They themselves were the one sacrifice: their lives, their lips and their possessions were daily to be offered to God for him to dispose of as he pleased. And the elements of the sacrifice were, firstly, unceasing verbal praise and thanksgiving; secondly, humility, hard work and good deeds; and thirdly, financial giving which impoverished their lives and enriched the lives of the needy. They could not choose between joyful praise and selfless generosity, or select humility instead of hospitality. A life either embraced all of these elements of sacrifice, or it wasn't a spiritual sacrifice at all.

Christ had taught his followers that they must renounce themselves and take up their cross daily: he hoped they would live their lives with exactly the same attitude as the man who has a very short life expectancy. Christ's clarion call 'follow me' is a bit like the First World War lieutenant's whistle which summoned his troops to follow him up the trench-ladder and 'over the top' into No Man's Land. No promises are made. The enemy is alert and dangerous. Casualties are inevitable. The first Christians knew that they followed the sacrificial Lamb who had been cut down in the prime of life; and they followed him knowing there was a very good chance that they would meet the same bloody end. Some did. Deacon Stephen was the first. The apostle James died about ten years later.

Luke fills 68 verses from Acts 6:8—7:60 with the details of Stephen's martyrdom, while James is clinically despatched in just one verse, Acts 12:2. It's as though martyrdom had become so commonplace in the first decade that Luke no longer considered it newsworthy. Peter's miraculous release, which immediately followed James' death, was obviously much more unusual and merited far greater attention than the summary execution of one of the original inner three disciples.

Imprisonment, persecution, punishment, hardship, rejection, suffering, and violent death were the lot of the first believers. And deaths occurred most frequently among those who witnessed to Christ most fervently. In time, the Greek word for witness, *martus*, became synonymous not with witness but with one who bore witness by his death. That small fact alone speaks volumes about the degree to which self-sacrifice was endemic in the early church.

Barnabas took an amazing risk in establishing the truth about Saul's alleged conversion (Acts 9:26–27). If Saul had been attempting to infiltrate the believers Barnabas would have been the first to be arrested. Peter took an equal risk when he sampled Cornelius' hospitality (Acts 10). If his vision had been a day-dream, instead of a message from God, he might have been excommunicated by his fellow leaders. But if neither of these two men had been prepared to sacrifice their reputations in the way that they were, the history of the church would have been quite different. God not only loves our sacrifices, he depends on them.

Just before his arrest Jesus had taught the disciples that nobody could have greater love than the man who lays down his life for his friends (John 15:13). And in Gethsemane he showed that 'friends' included people like Judas Iscariot. God's perfect and inexhaustible love so filled and so affected the first Christians that, like Jesus, they were ready to sacrifice themselves for their friends. At times this meant their own physical death; sometimes it meant the death of their reputation, more usually it meant the total sacrifice of their personal resources. But no matter what form it took, truly a spirit of self-sacrifice dominated the early church. Our Christian forefathers' deep personal allegiance to Christ and devoted commitment to each other caused them to be men who delighted to cry, 'death to Self'—and to mean it.

Worthless Sacrifices

Christ has expressly made wholehearted self-denial a condition of discipleship, which is to affirm that it is an essential attribute of holiness or love. But when men deny themselves with an ultimate reference to their own glory and happiness they are in fact only a spirit of self-indulgence and self-seeking. They are making good to self the end.

Charles Finney

The scriptural records of mankind and the church both begin with the discovery that God does not accept and reward every sacrifice made by men. Cain brought some of the produce of the soil as an offering for God, only to find that God was singularly unimpressed with his gift. Ananias and Sapphira presented part of the proceeds from the sale of their property to the first church leaders, and were confronted with God's displeasure. All three were severely judged by God because they had made sacrifices which he considered to be worthless and quite unacceptable: Cain became a social outcast, Ananias and Sapphira dropped dead.

It seems that the only sacrifices which God rewards with the blessing of his glory are those that have been motivated by selfless love; and I think that this is because his own sacrifice, which is the ultimate sacrifice and model for all sacrifice, was motivated solely by such love. Selfless love caused God to send his Son to die. Selfless love caused Christ to deny himself and take up his cross. And this selfless love was not only for God's friends and unfortunate but innocent sufferers, it was also for his enemies. Not even the slightest hint of self consideration tainted God's sacrifice: he did not give his Son to turn people into his personal slaves or to receive great acclaim, but because he knew that by his sacrifice he could secure a greater good for all creation. Selfless love always gives everything and expects nothing in return.

Christ's death was the lesser of two evils. His rejection and suffering, terrible though they were, were deemed by God to be less of an evil than the eternal sufferings of sinners. And this consideration induced God to sacrifice himself, even though it was for his enemies. God's sacrifice achieved nothing for himself, but because it could secure a greater good for the whole world the high personal cost was worthwhile.

Paul taught, in 1 Corinthians 13:3, that 'If I give away all that I possess, piece by piece, and if I even let them take my body to burn it, but am without love, it will do me no good whatever.' And much today that passes for self-denial and appears to be sacrificial is, in fact, only a specious form of self-indulgence that does the person no eternal good: the motivation is not undiluted self-denial, it is tainted with self-interest; selfless love is lacking.

A man might give up a highly-paid job to become a minister because he has always wanted to be a minister. A couple may sell their colour television set and give the money to the poor because they estimate that they will have a happier home without the box. A family might go without holidays for several years so that they can make a longed-for pilgrimage to Israel. Behind the Iron Curtain or in South Africa a martyr may perform a grand deed which he knows will mean his imprisonment or death because he wants to gain a place in the history books. Now when such apparent sacrifices are made with an ultimate reference to the person's own well-being or satisfaction, though the actions may be praiseworthy in themselves, they are still worthless sacrifices which will not be rewarded by God with his glory. When self is not denied the deeds can not be considered to be sacrifices in the true sense of the word.

Some people deny self in one form only to gratify self in another form. A minister may work hard, get up early, go to bed late, deny himself and his family in all manner of ways, apparently live a life of unceasing loving sacrifice, only to find that his sacrifice is unrewarded by God because it was motivated by the desire for human esteem. If the reason behind the sacrifice was the minister's wish for a good reputation then it is quite worthless: the man's name could easily be Ananias.

Another minister may work all hours of the day and night. He may sincerely love the people he serves, be successful, respected and loved. Yet if the real reason for his sacrifice is that he can't stand his wife and so spends as much time away from her as possible, his sacrifice is worthless and will not be rewarded by God.

A third man may work equally hard and will again, apparently, be an obvious living sacrifice, admired and imitated by many around him. Yet he will also miss out on the glory which is the heavenly reward for those who make earthly sacrifices if his sacrifices were made out of a sense of duty rather than of undiluted love. Such a man is no different from the Pharisees condemned by Jesus.

And another minister may have grasped the scriptural teaching about sacrifice and ruthlessly deny himself everything in the hope of obtaining a glorious eternal reward, without realising that he is as selfish and self-centred as the man who sacrifices the glory of eternity to enjoy the pleasures of earth. Sacrifices may be rewarded with glory but they should not be made to earn glory;

they should be made out of selfless love.

We know that if we love anybody more than ourselves we will always deny ourselves when our own interests clash with theirs. Parents love their children, and because of their love they deny themselves for their children's good. But my problem is that my self-denial is wrapped in self-gratification. Sometimes I make sacrifices for my four children because I derive enormous pleasure from seeing my children prosper. Now such satisfaction is far from wrong, but my apparent self-denial needs to be recognised as self-gratification and not misinterpreted as self-sacrifice. My earthly pleasure in my children's progress is my reward; heavenly glory is reserved for those who make real sacrifices. And any supposed sacrifice which is not rooted in selfless love is not a real sacrifice.

So often our love is not purely selfless. We want to do good for others not only for their benefit, but also as a means of achieving our own happiness or satisfaction. Men will often deny themselves for their families, their neighbourhood, their company, their country, or anybody or anything that involves them personally. The ultimate reason for their sacrifice is their personal interest in the benefit attained, so although their love appears to be selfless it is, in fact, quite selfish.

Many people have given large sums of money to famine relief in the last few years. They saw horrific pictures on television of human misery in Ethiopia and emptied their wallets in response. But did they give to gratify their feelings of compassion? To ease their consciences? To stop the misery which offended their eyes? To keep up with a new fashion? To reach a financial target? Or because they selflessly loved those who were hungry?

The starving are fed, whatever the reason for the giving. But what God wants from his people is self-denial, self-death and self-sacrifice which is motivated only by selfless love.

Most of the glorious dead we remember on Remembrance Sunday, unlike God, did not sacrifice themselves for their enemies: their motives were a mixture of self-denial and self-interest. And many of those who offer God a sacrifice of praise every Sunday do so out of an equivalent muddle of self-denial and self-indulgence. The praise they offer is the praise they like offering. The form of service they use is the one they prefer. They have their favourite songs and their favourite preachers. People are encouraged to feel comfortable. They are not urged to make sacrifices. If they feel good at the end of the service they comment to each other how the worship was really good that day. And all this is justified by the assumption that what the people want to offer God must be exactly what God wants to receive. The starving may be grateful for food from any source, but the glory of God is revealed only when sacrifices have been offered to him in disinterested selfless love.

When Moses confronted Pharaoh he told him that the form of sacrifice that the Israelites would offer to God had to be determined by God himself. Jesus was no ascetic who got some sort of perverse pleasure out of enduring hardships for their own sake, instead, he was a man who was motivated both by compassion for the needy and also by his Father's clear instructions. Sometimes, as in John 11:6, the sacrifice asked for by God was that Jesus do nothing even though human compassion must have urged immediate action. But at other times, as in Luke 7:11–15, compassion alone was the force behind Jesus' words and deeds.

God's selfless sacrifice on the cross was motivated by compassion because he knew that it was the only way by which sinful humans could be saved. Christ's love-inspired death was the only possible means of atonement for the sin of all mankind. Were it not for this sacrifice we would have been condemned to eternal punishment, and there would have been no escape. But this is hard for us to acknowledge. We do not like facing up to the seriousness of our sin and our total indebtedness to the cross. Some people proudly go to hell preferring to endure their own punishment than be humiliated by having somebody else bear it in their place. However, the truth is that we are all impotent. We may wish that there was something we could do. But there isn't. We might crave to be able to make some contribution to our own salvation. But we can't. We may look for ways of making amends to God for his suffering at Calvary. But we search in vain. Some believers foolishly fill their lives with all sorts of worthless sacrifices for this very purpose: they pray, they worship, they fast, they attend meetings and special events, they read books and listen to tapes, they give money—all with the hope that it will help with *their* salvation.

Graceless legalism has always been the hairshirt of the church. Earlier this century a new convert was told that if he was to be a Christian there were certain things which he must *not* do. But today the flourishing classes for new converts often give the opposite impression— that there are certain things which they *must* do: they *must* be baptised, they *must* become members of a particular congregation, they *must* tithe, they *must* not miss meetings, they *must* obey the elders, they *must* have a ministry, and so on, and so on. Tragically it seems to me that a generation of Christians is being reared which understands little of unconditional forgiveness and even less of salvation by grace alone, a generation which often unwittingly thinks that their self-denial is in some way necessary for their salvation.

The ritual sacrifices of the Old Testament were not all made for personal atonement or to appease an angry God: the majority were offered to God as an act of thanksgiving or dedication. And today we need to understand our giving, our obeying, our ministering in a similar way. We are not meant to give because we think we have to or because we think it will earn us any merit, but cheerfully, either in identification with those in need, or in thanksgiving to God for his goodness.

Sadly a few believers appear to be consecrated to self-interest and self-gratification, but Jesus calls all his followers to deny self and to go on denying self every day. Selfishness always makes good to self the end of every choice, whereas self-denial is the exact opposite. This does not mean that we should make bad to self the end of any choice, rather that we should always choose good to others and good to God in preference to good to self. Because Christ continually calls us to follow him and live his cross-life of living sacrifice, we should ensure that our lives, both personal and congegational, are dominated by selfless love for others and for God, and that they are filled with sacrifices untainted by self-interest. Anything else is worthless and unrewarded.

Sacrifice
and
Suffering

*A Christian must suffer more than another man,
and a saint more than an ordinary person.*

St Augustine

Sacrifice and suffering are very closely related; for just as glory is sacrifice's most likely heavenly reward so suffering is its inevitable earthly price. Therefore the Scriptures offer the same promise of glory for those who endure suffering as for those who make selfless loving sacrifices.

At first sight there may appear to be two different forms of suffering: that which is the natural consequence of a man's sacrificial choice, and that which arrives uninvited and unwanted. Yet the distinction is immaterial, for voluntary and involuntary suffering both feel much the same. When men and women are distressed or in pain they are not over-concerned with ascertaining the cause of their agony, but with knowing how it is to be endured.

For many people Romans 8 is the glorious climax of the New Testament, yet it is a chapter all about suffering. In verses 16 and 17 Paul argues that the Holy Spirit and our spirit bear united witness that we are children of God; that because we are his children we are also his heirs; and that an indispensable part of this legacy is sharing in Christ's sufferings in order to share in his glory.

In one sense it could be argued that all Christ's sufferings were voluntary because they all followed on from his relinquishment of his heavenly position and his assumption of the frail human condition. But by becoming and being as all men are he embraced the reality of involuntary, unsought suffering. Christ may have freely chosen to endure suffering-in-general, but he had no control over which particular forms of suffering he had to endure. For Christ suffering was not simply the consequence of his faithfulness to God in fulfilling his calling, suffering was the calling he had to fulfil: Isaiah 53 makes this plain. And when Christ calls us to follow him he does not warn us that suffering might occasionally be involved for just a few; rather he asks all of us daily to pick up our cross, on the understanding that suffering is the very nature of following him.

I think that suffering has six distinctive elements: rejection, disappointment, loneliness, poverty, pain, and dying (not death, for that is the end of all suffering for those who die in Christ). And Christ embraced all these aspects of suffering. He was—and still is—rejected by most people. He had—and still has—the disappointment, first, of seeing so few forsake all and follow him, and, second, of seeing even some of these few betray him. He often experienced loneliness—in the wilderness, for example; when his best friends could not stay awake to pray with him, and, above all, on the cross. He was homeless, he lived rough, he had no money, and he depended on the generosity of others for shelter, food and clothing. His body was racked with pain at his torture and execution. He died slowly, knowing all the time that he was dying and that hell was his first destination when he did die. And these six elements of his suffering are part of the glorious inheritance given to the heirs of God—you, me, the members of our western congregations, and our third world brothers and sisters.

The first letter of Peter is often called the epistle of suffering. As we have seen, it was sent from Rome at the outbreak of Nero's terrible persecution by Peter, Mark and Silas to groups of believers in what is modern-day Turkey. Peter's Christian friends in Rome were fodder for the Emperor's lions, and 1 Peter was sent to strengthen, comfort, and encourage those Christians who were not yet suffering in this way, but probably would be quite soon.

Throughout 1 Peter constant allusion is made to Isaiah 53, underlining the fact that all believers are followers of the Suffering Servant. 1 Peter 1:11 mentions the link between Christ's sufferings and his glory; 2:21 affirms that Christ's suffering is the example for believers to follow; and 4:13 urges those who can share in Christ's sufferings to be glad because it means they will enjoy a much greater gladness when Christ's glory is revealed. But more then this, 1 Peter includes six general principles about suffering which are fundamental to the way a Christian sees and endures both unsought suffering and the suffering which stems from selfless sacrifice.

Firstly, God allows our suffering: 1 Peter 3:17 and 4:19 repeat this basic Old Testament understanding (eg Job 1; Isaiah 14; and Amos 3) of suffering. Even though Satan has the power to make men suffer, they only suffer in the hand of God, for it is God who controls and allows suffering. It has always been difficult to relate this to God's love and justice, even though it is recognised that suffering does sometimes correct people, or purify them, or bring them into a closer relationship with God. Often those who suffer feel that God has lost control or forgotten them, so in 4:19 Peter urges those who are suffering 'to trust themselves to the constancy of the creator'. Again this repeats the familiar Old Testament idea that those in difficulty or danger find particular help in 'the name of Yahweh who made heaven and earth'. And in Romans 8:20–23 everything that God has made is seen to be part of this on-going struggle with corruption and suffering which was inaugurated by God. We are called, somehow, to trust that he who made us in the first place is still in absolute control; and that our Maker will bring us through the suffering, help us understand his eternal purposes, and reward us with a glory so great that the suffering will pale into complete insignificance.

Secondly, our suffering is ordinary. Peter writes, in 4:12, 'My dear people, you must not think it unaccountable that you should be tested by fire. There is nothing extraordinary in what has happened to you.' We in the twentieth century western church have been so cocooned that we especially need to grasp this fact. Suffering is meant to be the ordinary condition of those who follow the Suffering Servant of God; it is supposed to be supremely normal; and I guess that if selfless sacrifice dominated our congregations suffering would soon become quite commonplace. Some ministers today consider sufferers to be subnormal; they deem them problems; they make them feel that they are at variance with the Christian norm; they even sometimes find them an embarrassment—a negative comment on their own ministerial ability. Yet suffering, in whatever of the six forms it is experienced, ought to be unremarkable: our congregations should be packed out with people sharing the sufferings of Christ. I suspect that it is time we started educating ordinary believers about the Christian ordinariness of rejection, disappointment, loneliness, poverty, pain and dying. I feel that we need to show Christians how to embrace these elements of suffering, not avoid them. And I think that we need to teach believers that the reason why suffering should not be feared or shunned is because, as Peter states in 4:13, 'If you can have some share in the sufferings of Christ, be glad, because you will enjoy a much greater gladness when his glory is revealed.'

Thirdly, our suffering is a privilege and blessing. 1 Peter 3:14 states, 'If you do have to suffer for being good, you will count it a blessing.' And in Philippians 1:29 Paul writes, 'He has given you the privilege not only of believing in Christ, but of suffering for him as well.' Sadly, this is not how we normally view suffering today. We feel sorry for ourselves when we suffer. We do not count ourselves blessed. Like Job's friends we frequently wonder why a person is suffering, without ever realising that, like Job, it is probably because he is extremely virtuous. Peter goes on in 3:15 to urge his readers, 'Simply reverence the Lord Christ in your hearts, and always have your answer ready for people who ask you the reason for the hope that you all have.' Peter knew from personal experience in Nero's Rome that nothing causes unbelievers to ask more questions than believers who suffer well. It is still the same today: the ones who are sought out and listened to are not those who have been miraculously healed but those who have miraculously suffered: the Corrie Ten Booms and Joni Earicksons of the church. We need to recognise that those who are suffering are potentially our most potent evangelists. We need to teach them not to be ashamed of their suffering but to consider it a blessing and privilege, and urge them to get their evangelistic answers ready fast.

Fourthly, our suffering is shared with Christ. Throughout the New Testament the sufferings of the saints are always perceived as a sharing in the sufferings of Christ. This means not only that we share his sufferings, but more importantly that he shares ours. In Philippians 3:10 Paul wrote that he longed to know the power of Christ's resurrection 'and to share his sufferings by reproducing the pattern of his death'. And in Colossians 1:24 he suggests that his sufferings in some way 'complete what is lacking in Christ's afflictions for the sake of his body, that is, the church' (RSV). Peter hopes, in 4:13, that his readers can share in Christ's sufferings, and in 4:1 he tells those who are suffering to 'Think of what Christ suffered in this life, and then arm yourselves with the same resolution that he had.' Spiritual integrity demands that we go on reminding people that we are 'in Christ' and that the Spirit is 'in us'. Therefore whenever we suffer there must inevitably be a real fellowshipping with Christ and the Spirit in our sufferings; and that surely means they can be relied upon to help us to cope with our suffering with their firm resolution and uncomplaining silence.

Fifthly, our suffering is not unique. In 5:9 Peter tells his readers to remember that their brothers all over the world are suffering the same things, and he seems to suggest that this knowledge will give them as much comfort as their faith in Christ. Some sufferers seem to long for their difficulty to be unique; a few appear to obtain a macabre pleasure out of the attention which comes with novel symptoms or rare problems. But for most believers their suffering is compounded by bewilderment as to why they have been singled out for what appears to them to be special suffering. Such people need to grasp the essential ordinariness of their suffering, and to remember that across the world they have hundreds of thousands of brothers and sisters who are enduring exactly the same hardship. One of the problems with the unfortunate recent congregational emphasis is that this vital remembrance has been made much more difficult.

And sixthly, our suffering is brief. Peter states in 5:10, 'You will have to suffer only for a little while.' It should be noted, as Peter admits in 2 Peter 3:8, 'that with the Lord "a day" can mean a thousand years, and a thousand years is like a day', and I think Peter means that our suffering is always brief from an eternal perspective. God sees our suffering as the merest dot in the unceasing line of eternity. He knows that our suffering is temporary and temporal, but that our glorious reward is eternal and permanent. Paul grasped this truth, and put it neatly in Romans 8:18, 'I think that what we suffer in this life can never be compared to the glory, as yet unrevealed, which is waiting for us.' God only allows some of us to share in Christ's sufferings for a few days now and then; he gives others this privilege for several decades without apparent pause. But even the Christian man or woman who suffers alone in agony for eighty years should recognise the essential brevity of their suffering compared to the length and intensity of their promised eternal glory.

Peter ends his epistle of suffering in 5:10–11 with this absolute promise which I suspect is based on his observations of suffering believers in Nero's Rome: 'The God of all grace who called you to eternal glory in Christ will see that all is well again: he will confirm, strengthen and support you. His power lasts for ever. Amen.' All Christians are called to suffer; for some it will mean the unsought pain of cancer or bereavement, for others the voluntary pain of persecution or sacrificial poverty, and for still more it will involve the agony of impotence as they watch their unbelieving relatives die. But no matter what form of suffering a Christian is called to endure, regardless of whether it stems from sickness or sacrifice, Peter's principles and promises stand firm. Suffering is God-allowed; it is not extraordinary; it is a privilege and blessing; it is a sharing with Christ in his suffering; it is a sharing with the sufferings of all others joined to Christ around the world; and it is temporary. Soon it will be replaced by eternal glory.

*Glory
in the
Church Today*

Almighty Father,
whose Son was revealed in majesty
    before he suffered death upon the cross:
give us faith to perceive his glory,
that we may be strengthened to suffer with him
and be changed into his likeness, from glory to glory;
who is alive and reigns with you and the Holy Spirit,
one God, now and for ever.

Collect for the transfiguration of our Lord in the
Church of England's Alternative Service Book.

Again and again the Old Testament prophets, especially Isaiah and Ezekiel, cried out for God's glory to fill or cover the whole earth. They longed for God to show his character and presence to all creation. They pleaded for all men to see God's absolute holiness. They ached for the full extent of God's regal authority, beautiful perfection and magnificent power to be on permanent display. But until the death of Christ they cried in vain.

At Calvary God's glory shone even more brightly than ever the ancient prophets had dared hope, for the cross was the complete self-revelation of God's divine nature. There at Calvary God's own selfless sacrifice fully revealed his absolute holiness and infinite love, for Christ's sacrificial death was the supreme manifestation of God's character and presence. Without a doubt the cross was the quintessence of glory.

This glory is our destiny. It is what we were all made for; it is what we have all fallen short of; and it is what the death of Christ has once again made possible. Glory is the church's birthright. Glory is what God holds up before us all. But it is the glory of the cross: it is a glory-in-sacrifice.

God's great desire is for his church—you, me, our western congregations and our third world brothers and sisters—to fill the world with his glory. He longs for us together to reveal his character and presence to all creation. He aches for us corporately to radiate his absolute holiness and infinite love. He yearns for us openly to display his regal authority, beautiful perfection and magnificent power. And he calls us all to show all this, as he did at Calvary, in selfless sacrifice.

The sacrifices which God wants from his people are not ascetic, masochistic or suicidal; they are not awful calamities or ghastly accidents; they are not last-ditch gestures made to earn forgiveness or to atone for sins. The sacrifices God wants are the natural fruit of personal and congregational commitment to his suffering serving Son; they are the inevitable consequence of compassionate identification with the needy everywhere; and they are the glorious God-appointed beginning of abundant life with Christ.

We have seen that sacrifice began with God in Eden. There he set the standard of high personal cost which was followed by men as they offered him the best that they had in thanksgiving, dedication and commitment. In the desert he laid down the pattern of ritualistic blood sacrifices which his chosen people faithfully followed in worship for hundreds of years. Later, through his prophets, he pleaded for a sacrificial lifestyle of justice, compassion, and generosity to be wedded to the temporarily-atoning sin and guilt offerings of the Temple. Then, in Christ, he showed how sacrifice is the secret of fruitfulness, and instructed all who wanted to follow him to evidence this by clothing the naked, feeding the starving, visiting the prisoners, welcoming strangers, denying themselves daily, taking up their cross, and being ready to lay down their lives for people like Judas Iscariot.

Finally, he summed it up through his apostles by saying that the sacrifice he wanted was a life of unceasing praise, enduring good works, and the realistic sharing of personal resources.

It seems to me that the small part of the church to which I belong, the evangelical and charismatic section, began to rediscover the sacrifice of praise during the nineteen seventies. During that decade unspeakable joy usurped sober reverence as the chief characteristic of Christian services. Orchestras replaced organs. Hugs and hallelujahs, spontaneity and silence, clapping and dancing all emerged. A liturgical revolution took place. The 1 Corinthians 12 spiritual gifts were reclaimed and developed. Sankeys *Songs and Solos*, CSSM choruses and *Ancient and Modern* all gave way to *Sounds of Living Waters*, *Fresh Sounds*, *Mission Praise*, *Songs of Fellowship*, and *Hymns for Today's Church*, as thousands of new hymns and choruses were written and hundreds of old ones were modernised. Praise became a new and delightful priority.

It also appears to me that during the nineteen eighties this same section of the church seriously began to embrace the sacrifice of good works. The fear of 'the social gospel' was largely exorcised. Newer evangelical societies like Turnabout, Prison Fellowship, and CARE Trust started to do excellent caring work with homosexuals, prisoners, and unmarried mothers. Evangelical congregations became deeply involved with issues like abortion and unemployment, issues that fifteen years ago would have been considered the preserve of Roman Catholicism and the liberal wing of Methodism. Evangelistic coffee-bars, with tracts on every table and a sermonette at fifteen minute intervals, gave way to playgroups for mothers and toddlers, drop-in-centres for the unemployed, and lunch-clubs for the elderly, where meeting needs in as relevant and practical a way as possible is the first priority, and questions about Christ are not answered before they have been asked.

But despite the considerable impact of devastating television pictures and the prophetic writing of Ronald Sider the sacrifice of shared resources has not obviously been offered by any section of the western church. Perhaps this will begin to happen in the nineteen nineties; but how many more of our African brothers and sisters will have starved to death by then?

This is not to say that there is little concern for the poor. Far from it. Charitable giving has increased; but it will remain paternalistic and limited for as long as we only give money to the poor to the extent that our lifestyles are not noticeably affected. In the early church the rich sold their possessions and gave their money to a common fund which cared for all equally. In today's church we, the western rich, like our wealthy pagan friends, carry on getting richer while our poorer brothers go on getting poorer. We have elected to embrace a lifestyle which is indistinguishable from the selfish world around us. Surely we should inform ourselves about national and world average incomes, compare them with our own, and admit that there is a prima facie case for giving any excess to those with less. Surely we should live in such a way that we do not take more than our share of God's provision for the world. Surely the biblical standard for believers is 'enough', and everything we earn or own above this should be given to those with less than enough. The question we need to ask ourselves is not how much do I give to others, but how much do I keep back for myself? Jesus commended the widow's mite, not the rich man's gold. Perhaps an even more important question is how much do I love the needy? The incarnation and the crucifixion are my only acceptable measures.

I have to confess that I have found it very hard to begin to appreciate the significance of 'sacrifice', and even harder to start to implement it! For the last twenty years the church has emphasised self-fulfilment in Christ rather than self-denial with Christ. It has rarely questioned society's obsession with improving the standard of living. It has called homosexuals, adulterers and fornicators to repentance, but not the ambitious, the self-assertive, the argumentative, the rich, and the proud: just imagine what a witch-hunt there would have been if the Bible had condemned homosexuality as much as it condemns ambition!

I have been called to 'involvement', but never to 'sacrifice'. I have been told I must be committed to the leaders and to the congregation, but never to the starving and the naked. I have been implored to attend meetings, to study the Bible, to pray, to tithe, to raise my hands, to heal the sick, to attend to congregational business, but never to sell my possessions and give the proceeds to the poor. I have been told to win the world for Christ, but not to die for the world with Christ. I still cringe at my title for this trilogy: 'The death of Self' because it seems so old-fashioned and so unpalatable, yet I remain convinced that it is Christ's perennial cry to his beloved church.

For me the mystery was only unlocked when I finally grasped Christ's teaching that sacrifice is always the secret of fruitfulness. I had always known that 'the blood of the martyrs is the seed of the Church'. I had studied the early monastic movements and seen how dynamic spiritual communities and so much else that we value in society sprang out of unimaginable, deliberate hardships. I had read how men like Ferrer, Xavier, Zinzendorf and Wesley transformed the church and the world of their day by their selfless love-inspired sacrifices. I had been reared on a diet of nineteenth-century evangelical missionaries who landed in Africa with a life expectancy of only a few months. But I had never applied any of these examples to the detail of my own life and my own congregation.

Before any seed can multiply it must die and cease to be; if it seeks to preserve its independent existence it remains a single grain, but if the seed dies and disappears it yields a rich harvest. It was true for Christ. And it is true for those who follow him. Self-preservation leads to nothing except the preservation of self. Self-death leads to glorious growth and multiplication. Our calling in Christ is to die to ourselves on behalf of others. This is the true love and pure worship which God desires. It is also a phenomenal risk.

Faith was first linked to sacrifice with reference to Abel. And ever since then it has always taken faith to offer God our self as a sacrifice. But if we do risk everything, and if we do die to self for others, then we will surely discover that the death of self is never the end. The cross might be the universal symbol of our Christian faith, but the empty tomb is always before us. God will raise us up in this life to a wonderful new life of loving. He will reward us with his character and presence. He will use us to show the world his absolute holiness and infinite love. He will reveal through us his regal authority, his beautiful perfection, and his magnificent power. God's glory will fill that little bit of the earth where we live. There will be glory in the church. And, when we finally join him in eternity, God will give to us our glorious reward—which will more than make amends for all the suffering of our sacrifice.

Christians are not meant to be ambitious people. We are not meant to be individualistic people. We are not even meant to be nice people. We are just meant to be a company of suffering, self-sacrificing people who, together, exhibit all the redeeming marks of Christ so that they can be clearly seen by the world. We are meant to be a people who go on renouncing our selves and carrying our God-appointed crosses. We are meant to be those who complete what is lacking in Christ's afflictions for the sake of his body, that is, the church. We have been called to follow Christ, to suffer with Christ, and to suffer with all others who suffer in this life. And we are destined to share God's glory, his dazzling glory-in-sacrifice.

There would have been no resurrection without the cross. There will be no lasting renewal without the cross-life. And there can be no revival without selfless sacrifice. As Paul said, 'For me to live is Christ, to die is gain.'